The Invention
of Everyday Life

a poem

Lawrence Raab

Spuyten Duyvil

New York City

"The Invention of Everyday Life" first appeared in *Plume*.

ISBN 978-1-963908-33-6

Cover photograph by the author

Library of Congress Control Number: 2024945834

for Harriet Chessman & Bryan Wolf

THE INVENTION OF EVERYDAY LIFE

1.

A few days later Pierre arrived.

We strolled across the lawn
down to the lake. "Yesterday,"
he said, "she told me everything—
all the evasions and deceptions.
What should I believe?"

"Too often," I said, "people don't
feel the way we want them to feel."

"Too often," Pierre replied, "they pretend
not to understand. Too often someone
has to say, 'That person over there
is the one you should love.'
A friend might have told her.
You might have."

"Perhaps," I replied, unhappy
to find myself in the story.
I'd been expecting
more specific suspicions—when,
for example, and with whom?

But Pierre's attention
had strayed across the water,
drawn by something I couldn't
make out. We stood where we were,
waiting. Then he said:

"You own this lake, don't you?
I'd like to own a lake."

2.

You want to know what it's like
to be hopelessly lost?

At every moment we were afraid.
The fire of the sun burned away
the past and consumed our souls.

The color of the earth became
the color of the sky and then

of the air we had to struggle
to breathe. Huge anthills
surrounded us. I tried not to picture
what lived inside them.

We thought we were dead.
Everything we saw we saw
for the last time.

3.

So begins the explorer's account
of that long and harrowing expedition.

Reader, he writes, *be assured*
that before I set down one
sentence of the book you now hold
in your hands, I waited—

even longer than my doctors
advised—until I was sure
I was sane. And then

I saw what had escaped me:

how completely
I'd been seduced by the idea
of our endeavor—

casting aside all the familiar
affections, risking everything
for a journey, a beautiful excuse
to re-invent our lives.

Was that the idea?
Only that?

4.

"A dark cave: twisting human
forms, convex mirrors, a carpet
emblazoned with flames,
walls painted colors I can only
call poisonous." So the critic

described—too harshly?—
a large installation by a young artist
overly enamored of the work
of Kurt Schwitters, a construction

which, like Schwitters's great
Cathedral, appeared to be a "monument
to the inward spiral," as well as
"a vast confusion of objects." Also,
quite simply, his home.

5.

"After she left," Pierre said,
"I wandered aimlessly around
that quaint hotel where we
would never spend the night.

You remember it.

I believe you stayed there
once or twice.
With your wife, perhaps?

And as I wandered I gazed out
at the tumultuous sea and attempted
to recall a poem
appropriate to the moment."

"Which one came to you?"
"None of them."

6.

Pale shimmer
of a lake or river, great swells
of an ocean not far away,
a small pool

in a circle of trees
even closer: all of it
trickery and deceit—

mere resemblances
stolen from our weakness
and our need. "Demons,"
someone whispered. "Sorcery."

I could feel myself vanishing.

"I want to die in my bed," one man said.
"I don't want to die at all," said another.

I said nothing, trying to ignore
the rustling sounds of the night,
which were, I suspected,
disturbances of my mind.

7.

"As if it were a metaphor,"
Pierre continued, "I watched
the sea. In what way
might it resemble me?"

He paused—was I
supposed to speak? "Well…"
I began. "It goes on,"
said Pierre. "The sea,

that is. In all of nature
only people live to make themselves
more vulnerable. That's a fact."

"It must be," I said.

"Frankly," Pierre added,
looking carefully
at me, "I just wanted to fuck her,

and now I never will. Once
might have been enough.

What do you think?"

8.

The Cathedral of Erotic Misery,
Kurt Schwitters's masterwork,
eventually took over almost all
of his house in Hannover, Germany.

He lived inside
what he had accumulated,
arranged, and rearranged,
as we all do, if not
with such determination.

Each day he added
twisted scraps of metal,
a broken toy, a pair
of cufflinks, the death mask
of his first son. Also: trash

from the street. And various
items belonging to his friends—
Mies van der Rohe's pencil,
Sophie Taeuber-Arp's brassière.

9.

Reality, a famous poet said,
is the opposite of the obvious.

Or else, the critic proposed,
reality is *only* the obvious,
what we see every day,

take for granted,
and therefore
no longer see, concealed

as so much of the world is
by its own appearance.

10.

"It's a miracle!" cried the old woman
who believed in miracles,
watching us that morning as we emerged
from the murderous waves of heat.

"They've returned! They're home!"

I thought I recognized her.
Later I was informed
that my mother had died
shortly after our departure.

11.

Following the tepid response
to his book, *Forms and Failures
of Perception*, the critic concluded

that at any moment in history
only a few people are brave enough
to change their minds.

What would Schwitters have advised?

—Not to be the kind of person
who cares.

"Eternity is the best policy,"
Schwitters once announced,
then laughed, adding:

"I don't believe in anything at all."
Which of course wasn't true.

12.

At the melancholy center
of his *Cathedral*, inside
the Great Grotto of Love,

a man and woman embrace
among many shiny broken
objects. He has no head,

she has no arms.
A child nearby
is telling them to be careful.

13.

Pierre was right about that hotel,
although I'd stayed there
only once with the woman
he hoped would love him.

It rained continuously.

She and I stood on the porch
watching the rain disappear
into the garden, listening
to the ocean beyond it. I felt

I was growing distant from myself.

She said: "Won't it be lovely
to remember this?"

"Yes," I replied,
and because I wasn't sure
what she meant, I repeated myself: "Yes—
even with the rain."

"Oh no," she laughed, "especially with the rain."

Then she took my hand,
and we went back to our room.

14.

According to an almost certainly
apocryphal story, Kurt Schwitters

had a brief affair in 1926
with Sophie Taeuber-Arp, the wife

of his friend and fellow artist,
Jean Arp. Schwitters was said

to have insisted that before
they made love Sophie slowly

undress while he watched.
She understood

this aroused him. Once
he asked to keep

the brassière she had just
unfastened, slipped off

her shoulders, and allowed
to fall beside the bed.

She refused.
Later he stole it.

15.

After we were released from the prison
of that desert, being alive
seemed wrong. I needed to forget

too much—the terrible weight of the sky
we had labored under, the cruel
hounding of the wind, and at night
maybe one dream flickering through

the past onto a blank page
from which we'd been erased.

16.

"You must try to forget me,"
said the woman Pierre had wished
to possess. They stood beside
the fountain in that hotel's
small but elegant garden. In fact,
Pierre loved her. In fact,
she had attempted
to return his feelings. But it's better
now, she told herself, for him
to believe in betrayal
rather than indifference.
She confessed to several recent affairs.
Her stories, however, were not
entirely true, there having been
only a single lover. "Listen,"
she said. "If the world
is as you suspect,
then it is." Whereupon
she pressed two fingers gently
against his lips, instructing him
in the art of acceptance.
He did not resist her touch,
wishing for the misery of that moment
never to end.

17.

As his *Cathedral* grew
Schwitters named its spaces:

The Cave of the Murderers.
The Cave of the Fallen Heroes.
The Cave of Friendship.

When more room was required,
he sealed up some of the oldest
grottoes and caves, although
everything inside remained

undisturbed—a box of pills
next to a lock of hair, the torn sleeve
of a shirt, a half-smoked cigarette—
relics, souvenirs. Hopeless
disarray, one visitor recalled.

We asked for details, but Kurt
just shrugged. "It is unfinished,"
he said, "out of principle."
So much had been nailed shut

and painted over, was it even
meant to fit together?—pencil stubs
and train receipts, a music-box
that played *Silent Night,*

the crushed head of a doll,
and flowers—*immortelles*—
suspended in a bottle of urine.
"After a while," Schwitters told
a friend, "some things

no longer need to be visible.
But they do not disappear.
They are all deep down inside."

18.

We'd been worn away:
pressing forward, stumbling
off in any direction
we hoped might lead us

away from where we were.
Failing, we asked: Is it time
to submit? Why not

walk calmly out into the dark
toward whatever has been
waiting to receive us?
Yet none of us did. Someone

nearby kept crying
and crying, unable to stop.
I can't say that wasn't me.

19.

"The world is doomed,"
the critic wrote,
hesitated, and started over.

"If the world is doomed,
what is the difference between
the decadent's retreat into sensuality
and the ascetic's rejection of the flesh?"

A flicker of light distracted him.

He walked over to the window
and was startled
to see in the park across
the street so many

complications of the same color—
green in motion, and green
poised and intent,
then afloat, released
from the leaf or blade

of grass it had been
attached to—green
shifting and converging
as if everything all at once
wanted to surprise
and persuade him,

though of what
he had no idea.

20.

A small collage hung above
the bed in our room. Heartbreaking,
one might have thought, if one had been
so inclined. I pointed it out.

"Lovely," she said, "but also
...incomplete."

"That's what makes it lovely," I replied.

She seemed surprised I would say
such a thing, and smiled.

Whenever she smiled like that
I was sure she would never
reveal her thoughts.

21.

I told her I recognized
that artist's work—he'd narrowly
escaped from the Nazis,

lived in exile, died
poor and unknown, but now—

"Tell me his name," she whispered,
"when it comes to you."

As we were leaving I asked
the owner if he knew
who had made that picture in our room.

"Céline," he replied. "My daughter.
When she was eight.
It's very pretty, isn't it?"

22.

Schwitters no doubt regretted
his affair with Sophie Taeuber-Arp.

He would not have wanted
to think of himself as a man
capable of betraying his friend.

Was she that beautiful?

No. Nor had it been
fate, or happenstance. Instead,
the critic thought:

a willful interruption of his life,

a way to step outside himself
and his sadness.

To feel without knowing,
Schwitters once claimed,
was the aim of his art.

23.

We wrote our books to be done with it.

But how different our stories had become.
There was no putting them together.

Perhaps the truth wasn't useful
anymore. No matter—

I doubt if any of my companions
found themselves
drawn back to that chaos
as I did.

And to look for what?

I returned, and escaped,
and returned—each night
more deeply lost.

Nothing was ever the way it was.

24.

The sky was unusually blue,
the lake was a mirror,
and the horizon continued
to pretend to be an invitation.

Pierre had departed early.

I wondered when I might
encounter him again.
And if that mattered to me.

He'd always been more
of a guest than a friend—
a little melancholy but agreeable
enough until he discovered
that the woman he loved

preferred me, after which
he would not stop insisting
we were clearly wrong
for each other, it would never

last, I was incapable
of caring for her.
Which was true.

But she had no desire to be cared for.

This Pierre did not understand.
Nor, at that moment, did I.

25.

Casting aside the familiar
allegiances, connecting
anything with anything else—
the ticket, the pencil,
the locomotive,

the scarf. Creating
a world from everything
this world refuses to save.
That was the idea.
Not to explain,
not to be certain.

In 1943, during one
of the allied bombings,
Schwitters's house in Hannover
was struck and his *Cathedral*
completely destroyed.

Art is a game, he'd written,
played with serious problems.

About such matters
who can expect
full understanding?

I leave things as they are
only I cover them.

26.

If the world is doomed,
does everyday life vanish?

Or is it all that remains?—
altered, reinvented,
eventually

taken for granted.

27.

Throughout the long autumn of that year
such questions plagued me.

"Come to bed," said my wife.
"Soon," I answered. "There's something
I'm trying to remember." "You won't,"

she said. "But if you do
it will have changed,
and you should know

you were the one who changed it."
I wanted to ask which part
of all of the past I could depend on,

but I suspected *None of it*
would be her answer. I pictured rain

falling into the sea. "Trust me,"
she said. "Where we are
is what we have. Think of Pierre,

poor boy, deceived by his friend.
Think of the story

of those explorers lost in the desert,
how in many versions they don't survive,
how in one they do."

LAWRENCE RAAB is the author of ten books of poems, including *Mistaking Each Other for Ghosts* (Tupelo, 2015), which was longlisted for the National Book Award and named one of the Ten Best Poetry Books of 2015 by *The New York Times*, and *What We Don't Know About Each Other* (Penguin, 1993), a winner of the National Poetry Series and a finalist for the 1993 National Book Award. His latest collection is *April at the Ruins* (Tupelo, 2022). *Why Don't We Say What We Mean?*, essays about poetry, appeared in 2016. He is the Harry C. Payne Professor of Poetry Emeritus at Williams College.